Letters From Lucy

Written by Moira Andrew
Illustrated by Rhian Nest James

Collins Educational
An Imprint of HarperCollinsPublishers

Dear Grandad,
 Get well soon. Mum and I are looking after Grandma until you get home.
 Love from
 Lucy
PS We are looking after Sammy too.

Dear Lucy,
    Thank you for your card.
It is on the locker beside my bed.
Thank you for taking care of
Grandma and Sammy for me.
        Love from
        Grandad

Dear Grandad,
    I wish I could have a ride in an ambulance. Was it fun? Sammy didn't eat his breakfast. I think he misses you.
              Love from
                Lucy

PS I miss you too.

Dear Lucy,
   The ambulance isn't as much fun as you think. Don't worry about Sammy. To tell the truth, I'm not very hungry these days either.
   Love from
   Grandad

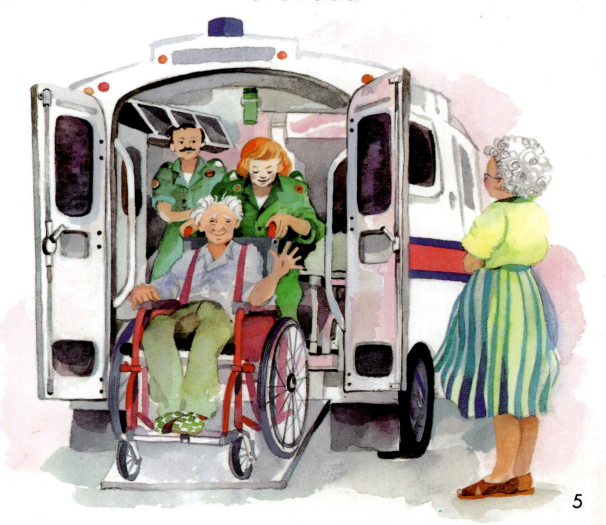

Dear Grandad,
   Sammy tried to catch a mouse today. It ran behind your chair. Mum and I put it outside.

   Love from
   Lucy

PS Grandma says you have a drip in your arm. Does it hurt much?

Dear Lucy,
   What a bad cat Sammy is! The drip makes me look like a robot, but it doesn't hurt much.
   Love from
   Grandad

Dear Grandad,
 I have watered all the plants in the greenhouse for you. Sammy ate all his tea.
Love from
Lucy
PS Please don't die, Grandad.

Dear Lucy,
 I'm doing my best not to die, but sometimes I feel very tired. Thank you for looking after the plants. You must be very busy.
Love from
Grandad

Dear Grandad,
   Sammy lost his collar today and we had to buy a new one. It is yellow and very smart.
   Love from
   Lucy

PS Grandma was crying so I gave her a big hug.

Dear Lucy,

Tell Grandma not to cry. I feel a lot better. We had a wheelchair race along the hall and the nurse sent us back to bed!

Love from
Grandad

Dear Grandad,

    Grandma says you are just like naughty boys! You made her laugh. Sammy slept on my bed last night.

        Love from
          Lucy

PS I got a new jumper yesterday. I wish you could see it.

Dear Lucy,

    That's two surprises for me when I get home, your new jumper and Sammy's new collar. I can hardly wait.

        Love from
        Grandad

Dear Grandad,
    Grandma was singing today and Sammy was chasing butterflies in the garden. We are all glad that you are getting better.

    Love from
        Lucy

PS Grandma says that they have taken the drip away.

Dear Lucy,

    Yes, I feel a lot better now. The nurses let me walk up and down the ward, but they still won't allow wheelchair racing! Tell Sammy I'll be home soon.

        Love from
        Grandad

Dear Grandad,
   Home tomorrow! Yippee! Grandma has dusted the house from top to bottom. I have a surprise for you. It's a WELCOME HOME card.

   Love from
   Lucy

PS I love you, Grandad.

Dear Lucy,

    Be a good girl and help Grandma find my clothes. She's so excited she is sure to forget something. Thank you for all your letters. They have helped to make me well.

                Love from
                Grandad

PS I love you too.